NEW WAYS
FOR LIFE ™

Youth Journal
Life skills for young people

This journal belongs to:

AUTHORS
Bill Eddy, LCSW, Esq.
Susie Rayner, Mediator

PUBLISHER'S NOTE

This publication is designed to provide accurate and authoritative information about the subject matters covered. It is sold with the understanding that neither the publisher nor the author are rendering legal, mental health, or other professional services in this book. If expert assistance, legal services or counseling is needed before making decisions that impact you, your children and your family, the services of a competent professional should be secured.

ISBN 978-1950057092

Copyright © 2020 by Bill Eddy and Susie Rayner

High Conflict Institute, LLC
7701 E. Indian School Rd., Ste. F Scottsdale, AZ 85251
www.highconflictinstitute.com

All rights reserved.

No part of this book may be used or reproduced, scanned, or distributed in any printed or electronic form whatsoever without the express written permission of the publisher except in the case of brief quotations embodied in critical articles and reviews. Failure to comply with these terms may expose you to legal action and damages for copyright infringement.

Book design: Julian Leon, The Missive

CONTENTS

A NOTE FROM US TO YOU	4
USING YOUR JOURNAL	5
THE 4 BIG SKILLS	6
HOW YOUR BRAIN AND BODY LEARN SKILLS	7
SKILL 1. MANAGING YOUR EMOTIONS	9
A. COPING WITH STRESS	10
B. CALMING YOURSELF	14
C. OUR BRAINS UNDER STRESS	20
D. ENCOURAGING STATEMENTS	26
E. EMOTIONS ARE CONTAGIOUS	32
F. GOAL SETTING FOR MANAGED EMOTIONS	36
SKILL 2. FLEXIBLE THINKING	41
A. THE PROCESS FOR FLEXIBLE THINKING	42
B. SOLVING PROBLEMS AND FLEXIBLE THINKING	46
C. "ALL-OR-NOTHING" THINKING OR FLEXIBLE THINKING?	52
D. WAYS OF USING FLEXIBLE THINKING	56
E. MAKING PROPOSALS	60
F. GOAL SETTING FOR FLEXIBLE THINKING	66
SKILL 3. MODERATE BEHAVIOR	71
A. AVOID OVERREACTING	72
B. MODERATE BEHAVIORS	76
C. SENDING TEXT MESSAGES & WRITING EMAILS	82
D. PRACTICE SENDING TEXT MESSAGES WITH BIFF	88
E. 10 BIFF RESPONSE QUESTIONS TO ASK YOURSELF	90
F. GOAL SETTING FOR MODERATE BEHAVIOR	96
SKILL 4. CHECKING YOURSELF	101
FEELINGS WORD GUIDE	116

A NOTE FROM US TO YOU

We know we can't tell you what to do and we can't (as the saying goes) put an old head on young shoulders. But what we can do is provide you with a set of skills that we wish we had when we were your age. Hindsight is a wonderful thing! We have often asked ourselves, "Would my teen years and school life have been different if I had known about these skills?"—ABSOLUTELY!

As you go through life, you will learn lots of new things, you will see amazing sights, you'll hopefully go to exciting places and experience different cultures. You will meet people that you absolutely love and adore, and they may be your best friend forever, or on the flip side, you will meet people that you just don't gel with—and that's OK. And sometimes you meet people you love, but they turn out to be people you don't gel with too. The skills we'll give you will help in dealing with that, so it turns out OK also. Life is waiting for you. However, it won't all be perfect.

You will be in situations that are stressful at times, sometimes you'll feel happy and content, nothing will be an issue. Sometimes you'll be somewhere in the middle!! Or maybe you'll be at the other end of the scale, like really sad, angry or frustrated. Do you sometimes feel that? We all do! That's why these skills are an absolute must for you! These skills are on a need to know basis and, you need to know them.

The skills that you will learn will help YOU feel in control. They will help you to cope with and deal with the good and the not so good times in your life—especially the not so good times.

We really hope that you take these skills and use them on a day to day basis until they become second nature. We will ask you "How easy is it to brush your teeth?" If you practice using these skills in your classrooms or at home or when you are playing sport, they will become automatic, just like cleaning your teeth.

We honestly wish you every success in your life.
A saying for you: *If it is to be, it is up to me!*

Pack these skills in your bag every day and off you go...
New Ways for Life!

A LITTLE ABOUT US

Susie lives in Mentone, Melbourne, Australia. Her love of Australia's High Country and the outdoors takes her to adventures with her husband, 2 teenage boys and their dog on camping trips. Her passion to help people in emotional turmoil and disputes is highlighted in her work as a mediator, dispute resolution practitioner and family conflict coach. In her work with families she realized that young people were missing vital life skills that were being taught at school and thus was born *New Ways for Life*.

Bill lives in San Diego, California, USA, near the ocean, but he's not a surfer. Instead, he likes to take walks by the ocean and to go backpacking and skiing in the mountains. For several years he was a Kindergarten teacher, then he became a youth counsellor and drug counsellor at a psychiatric hospital and outpatient clinic for 12 years. For the past 20 years, he has been a family lawyer and family mediator helping children, youth and parents going through separation and divorce by teaching skills and resolving conflicts along the way.

USING YOUR JOURNAL

BEFORE YOU START ON NEW WAYS FOR LIFE, WE WOULD LIKE TO EXPLAIN WHY YOU HAVE THIS JOURNAL.

THIS JOURNAL HAS BEEN PROVIDED TO YOU AS SOMETHING THAT IS PERSONAL AND CONFIDENTIAL.

It is something you can read back to yourself when you come up against difficult or stressful situations in your life. It's not complicated and there are no tests at the end. We know that you are learning lots at school, but we think there are some vital life skills that are in addition to the education that you are receiving. Not everything you learn at school will be used in your future, however, the New Ways for Life skills will be.

Learning these new skills will take practice, just like learning a musical instrument or learning to dance or learning to surf. We know you don't want to hear this but you know what they say, *PRACTICE MAKES PERFECT!*

THERE ARE TWO TYPES OF QUESTIONS IN YOUR JOURNAL

"HOW DID I DO?" QUESTIONS
These questions will get you to think about what you have done and how you have responded to situations in the past.

"WHAT CAN I DO?" QUESTIONS
These questions are about what you can do from this day forward with the information that you are learning. It is recommended that you complete each question so that you get the most out it.

THE COURSE TOPICS

MANAGING EMOTIONS
EMOTIONS ARE CONTAGIOUS
MODERATE BEHAVIOR
CHECKING YOURSELF

OUR BRAIN AND STRESS
FLEXIBLE THINKING
B.I.F.F RESPONSES

THE 4 BIG SKILLS

HERE'S WHY WE TEACH THESE IN THIS YOUTH JOURNAL.

1 MANAGING YOUR EMOTIONS

We teach managing your emotions because unmanaged emotions and intense emotions can push people away from us or distract us from what we really wanted to do and accomplish.

This is a big part of what you learn in the teenage years. Of course, some adults are still learning this too.

2 FLEXIBLE THINKING

We teach Flexible Thinking because "All-or-Nothing" Thinking isn't realistic in a lot of situations and it can really mess things up, even when we can't see it at the time. Flexible Thinking will really help in your future, because you will face situations that you have never faced before—and sometimes no one has ever faced before.

This will help you get along and come up with new ideas that fit new situations.

3 MODERATE BEHAVIOR

We teach moderate behavior because extreme behavior usually doesn't work and can mess up relationships with friends, family and jobs someday. This is another big part of growing up, getting along and solving problems.

Moderate behavior can make you likeable, respected and successful at what you want to do.

4 CHECKING YOURSELF

We teach checking yourself because we need to be aware of how we are managing our emotions, using flexible thinking and using moderate behavior.

It's easy to check everyone else and blame them for problems, but its more effective to check ourselves. Because we can't control others, but we can control ourselves.

HOW YOUR BRAIN AND BODY LEARN SKILLS

→ **WE ARE CONSTANTLY LEARNING SKILLS THAT WE CAN USE AGAIN IN THE FUTURE.**

Your brain has about 100 billion neurons that manage how you think, how you deal with feelings and how you behave. These neurons also build over a trillion connections to each other based on your life experience.

The more you practice a skill, the stronger the connections between the parts of the brain and your body that use these skills; and the easier it is to do it in the future automatically.

It's like a pathway in your brain when you first try a new skill. Then, the more you use it, the skill becomes like a road and then like a superhighway of neurons. So, practice is the key to learning and mastering skills. This is what sports stars do, what musicians do, what scientists do and what everyone does.

> **For example:** Imagine that you're learning to play the guitar. At first your fingers hurt when they're pressed against the strings, but you get used to it over time. You make mistakes when you play the strings as you get started. You're frustrated! Then you learn to play a chord. Yay! Then you learn another chord. Then you forget the first chord. But then you practice it again and it gets easier to remember.

That's what this Youth Journal is about and what adolescence is about. This is when you are learning the skills to become an adult and manage how you think, feel and act in the world to be the most effective you.

Fortunately, you have time to make mistakes and practice until these 4 Big Skills become automatic most of the time. In fact, you can learn a lot from making mistakes—we all do—so we will be encouraging all along the way.

Nobody's perfect at any of these skills. We just get better and better with practice.

SKILL 1

→ MANAGING YOUR EMOTIONS

A. COPING WITH STRESS

WHAT IS STRESS?
Stress is a natural human response to pressure when faced with challenging and sometimes dangerous situations. Stress doesn't have to control our lives.

If stress lasts a long time or overwhelms our ability to cope, it can have a negative effect on our health, well-being, relationships, work and general enjoyment of life.

Under stress, your body releases hormone chemicals like adrenaline and cortisol into your bloodstream to get you ready to fight, or to flee the situation, or to freeze and pretend you're not really there. Your muscles get tense, your brain narrows its focus and you get ready for action. If you're really in danger, your stress response helps you protect yourself.

Once you're away from the danger, then these chemicals leave your bloodstream until they're needed again and your body and brain calm down. Usually this all happens very quickly and you don't even need to think about it. It's automatic.

These upset feelings can come and go many times a day.

Writing Exercise #1
How have you handled your upset feelings?
Think of one time that you just acted on your upset feelings and the outcome it had. When you acted on these feelings, did they help solve the problem or did it make the situation worse?
Write down how it went for you.

How have you handled your upset feelings?

B. CALMING YOURSELF

One of the best things we can do to manage our emotions is to develop the ability to calm ourselves—especially in upsetting situations.

It's good to know that you can actually calm yourself down even if your brain and body have gone into a stress response. It usually takes a few minutes, but after you get used to it you can calm yourself down quite quickly.

It also depends on how dangerous the situation was or how intense your brain and body response was, so sometimes it takes a lot longer to calm down.

The body has a way of healing itself, even after a crisis. You can actually help yourself heal. On the next page there are a few methods you can use to calm your emotions when you want to or you need to.

Calming yourself will lead you to problem-solving, so that you don't slip into defensive reacting. Remember to be aware of calming yourself down first and then responding to a situation. If you calm yourself first, you will almost always make a wiser choice on how to deal with a situation.

METHODS YOU CAN USE

1. TAKE A BREAK
You can just go to your room or take a walk or focus on something else.

If you're in the middle of a conversation or an argument, it helps to say "I need to take a break. I'll talk to you later about this, like tomorrow."

If you're talking to someone you need to impress or cooperate with (like a parent or a good friend or your boss at a job), you may not be able to leave the conversation for long.

You could say: "Can you give me 5 minutes to think about this and then come back to this discussion?"

If they say "No," then try this next skill. They will be impressed that you can become calm even during an upsetting conversation.

2. TAKE SOME DEEP BREATHS
It's amazing that we can control how we breathe by thinking about it.

On its own, our breathing speeds up when we're upset, to get our body ready to fight, flee or freeze. But you can slow down your breathing in any upsetting situation without even telling anybody that you're doing this. This makes your whole body calmer.

Some people find it helpful to just count silently and slowly to yourself from one to ten, or backwards from ten down to one.

3. TALK WITH SOMEONE NEUTRAL
For this it helps to talk to someone who is not going to pressure you to do anything.

You want someone who will just listen. You can even tell the person to just listen for a few minutes while you get it off your chest. Tell them whether you just want some support or empathy (like: "Yeah, I can see how upsetting that is") or if you want suggestions (like: "Why don't you try this instead.")

You can even do this with others who are upset. Ask them if they want to tell you what's wrong and have you just listen, or if they want some suggestions.

When people are upset, they mostly just want someone to listen and care about them. When people rush to make suggestions it often upsets them even more.

4. GIVE YOURSELF AN ENCOURAGING STATEMENT
At any time, you can give yourself an encouraging statement.

Here's an example: "I know this sadness will eventually go away" or "I can do this, I've done it before."

We suggest that you think of an encouraging statement that you can tell yourself before you go into a difficult situation or discussion. For example: "What he's going to say is just about him, it's not about me." Or: "I can just listen respectfully without having to get defensive or try to prove anything."

Some people put post-it stickies around their room or on their bathroom mirror to remind themselves every day that they can feel good about themselves and what they're learning.

Writing Exercise #2
How have you calmed yourself?
Think about the last time you were sad or angry or frustrated. How did you eventually calm yourself down?

Writing Exercise #3
What can I do?
Think about ways you can calm yourself.

1. Write down a situation that might happen in the future, when you might need to take a break?

2. Write down which method you might use to calm yourself? Write why you picked that one?

3. Think of three neutral people you could call when you are upset. Write their names here.

1
2
3

C. OUR BRAINS UNDER STRESS

We don't always have a stress response when there's a problem. Our brains have two different types of responses to problems. It's like our brains really have at least two different brains within them to take care of different types of problems.

While they work together but one side (hemisphere) tends to dominate at a time.

LOGICAL BRAIN
(Generally Left Brain) This type of response includes examining details, looking at past solutions, looking at options for what to do now, planning for the future, asking questions, getting new ideas from books, videos or other people.

REACTIVE BRAIN
(Generally Right Brain): The right brain is where a lot of good things are processed, such as art, creativity, intuition, big picture ideas, interpretation of facial expressions, tone of voice and hand gestures. It's also where our fast defensive reactions are based. This type of response triggers our stress hormones and is usually fast, jumps to conclusions, shuts down our logical problem-solving, has a burst of energy, and drives us into fight, flight or freeze behavior. It is survival-oriented and doesn't think about the future. It's all about intensely dealing with right now, with quick action to save your life.

The idea is that both brain approaches are helpful and important. What matters most is which approach to use in each type of situation.

If we don't "think" about it, usually our brain automatically decides which approach to use. Sometimes your brain makes a mistake about this and over-reacts when you shouldn't or under-reacts when you should take quick action.

THIS IS A LOT OF WHAT ADOLESCENCE IS ABOUT
Teaching our brains to learn which situations are a crisis needing a fast reaction without thinking, and which situations are a logical problem to solve by looking at all of your options. You're forming pathways in your brain connecting neurons and strengthening your skills as you practice them. What you learn now will become automatic after enough practice.

STRESSFUL TIMES AND SITUATIONS
When you're in an upsetting or stressful situation, your Reaction Brain takes over and shuts down your Logical Brain. You go into defensive thinking, protection, fight, flight or freeze.

But sometimes you'll be in an ordinary situation or a slightly stressful situation that feels like a crisis. Then, when your Reaction Brain takes over it doesn't fit the situation. It might even make things worse or at least be embarrassing for a few minutes.

The goal is to realise when you're upset that you can control this intensity of emotions. You can shift yourself so your Logical Brain steps in and calms you down enough to start to solve problems.

Writing Exercise #6
How did you react/respond?

Think of a time when you were upset. What upset feelings did you have and did those feelings help you solve a problem or make it worse? This could be when you were told do something you didn't want to do, like clean up your room! Did you solve a problem or create a new one?

Think of a time when you were upset, but you were able to overcome your upset feelings to solve a problem.

Writing Exercise #7
What did you learn?
What was the most important information you learned about your brain – (What can one side do to another, that could cause you to not be able to solve a problem or make it worse?)

Writing Exercise #8
How can you use this new knowledge in your daily life?
Look at what you wrote down on above: Now you know that your Reaction Right Brain can technically shut off the Logical Left Brain.

D. ENCOURAGING STATEMENTS

Always have an encouraging statement in mind that you can use when you feel like you don't have control anymore. You don't have to say it out loud, you can say it quietly to yourself or silently inside your head.

HERE'S SOME EXAMPLES OF ENCOURAGING STATEMENTS YOU CAN GIVE YOURSELF

- I know I'm going to be ok... I'm strong and I'm smart.
- I'm not going to give up... I can do this.
- This will pass

Keep your encouraging statement positive and simple (so it's easy to remember).

Don't let any negativity slip into it, like comparing yourself to others or to things you don't like. For example

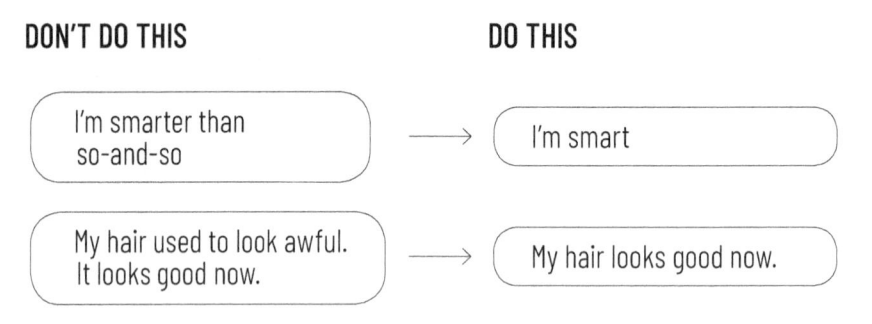

DON'T DO THIS	DO THIS
I'm smarter than so-and-so	→ I'm smart
My hair used to look awful. It looks good now.	→ My hair looks good now.

Writing Exercise #9
Encouraging statements by others

Think of some encouraging statements that other people have told you that made you feel better about an upsetting situation. Have a think. You may have even seen someone else calming themselves down in a stressful situation on TV or in a movie. Write some encouraging statements that you've heard before, below.

Writing Exercise #10
Encouraging statements of your own

Write down three encouraging statements you can tell yourself when you're upset in the future. You can used lessons you learned from past experience.

1

2

3

Writing Exercise #11
Planning ahead for encouraging statements under stress

Stressful Situation One: Now picture in your head a time in the next week when you might be facing a situation that's going to be stressful. It could be with anybody. A friend, a family member, someone in your neighbourhood or even at a job or volunteer group you're involved with. Write it down.

Encouraging Statement One: Next, picture yourself saying your encouraging statement in that situation, keeping yourself calm, listening, thinking, solving problems.
Remember, whatever the process, you are staying calm so you can think. That means you'll be using your problem-solving brain, instead of your defensive reacting brain.
Picture yourself using your encouraging statement. If the encouraging statement doesn't feel right for the situation, then think of a new one that would be. Remember to keep it positive and encouraging. Write down your encouraging statement here

Stressful Situation Two: Now picture in your head another time when you might be facing a situation that's going to be stressful. If you're having trouble of thinking of one, perhaps you could think of another one from the past. Write down the situation below.

Encouraging Statement Two: Under that stress, what encouraging statement can you tell yourself? Write it down below.

Preparation is the key

You're now prepared with at least two encouraging statements that you can use in the coming weeks if you find yourself in a stressful situation.

E. EMOTIONS ARE CONTAGIOUS

Just because someone is upset doesn't mean that you have to have the same feelings. Being aware of this means that you can have more control over your own emotions.

What happens is that one person's upset emotions instantly can trigger your own brain to have the same response. This helps a group of people suddenly take action in a crisis.

> **EXAMPLE**
> If there was a shark or a tidal wave suddenly coming close to shore where you were swimming, you might see people start running and shouting with very frightened faces, but too far away to hear what they were saying. Just their frightened faces would tell you that there was a real problem and you better start running too.

In fact, your Reaction Right Brain is so fast at sensing danger, you might find yourself running before you even realized why. Your Logical Brain is slower than your Reaction Brain—which is a good thing if you're in a crisis that requires very fast action.

> But **once you're running,** your Logical Brain might start figuring out where you should run to, to be in the safest place.

> But **if you were too terrified,** you might just follow the crowd and not use your Logical Brain at all.

The same thing can happen in social situations where it feels like your life is in danger even though it isn't. Maybe a friend of yours is terribly upset. It could suddenly feel like you were in danger or should feel very upset too.

EXAMPLE

> I'm so angry with John. You know what he said to me? He said _____. Don't you just hate him for saying that?

But maybe you don't feel the same way. You shouldn't have to "just hate John" now because your friend does.

You have a right to have your own feelings about everything. Or to decide how you want to feel.

Writing Exercise #12
How did it feel to be put in this situation?

Think of **two examples** in which someone wanted you to feel the same way they felt. Maybe that person was sad or angry and they wanted you to feel that way too.
How did it feel to be put in this situation? Write it down below.

Writing Exercise #13
Picking up on others' emotions

Example: Your friend Sally told you not to talk to Emily because she thought that Emily had been talking about Sally behind her back. Your friend said: "I don't like Emily anymore for saying what she said. I'm not going to be friends with her, and I don't want you to be friends with her either." Right away you notice that you start feeling angry at Emily too. You absorbed her emotions.

In this situation with Sally and Emily, write down what you could do to avoid picking up Sally's feelings.

Sample answer to the above: There's no one right answer, but here's an example of what you could say to yourself: "I can understand that Sally might be really upset about this. But I don't know if what Emily said is even true. Emily has done nothing to me. What's my view on this? I actually don't hate Emily. Just because Sally is upset, it doesn't mean that I have to be upset or act any different towards Emily.

Write down a new example like this of when you picked up the feeling another person was having? Was it when you were playing sport, in the classroom, at home, in the car?

Write down what you could tell yourself in your new example, so you could have your own feelings.

F. GOAL SETTING FOR MANAGED EMOTIONS

The process of setting goals is to allow yourself to choose where you want to go and what you want to achieve. By knowing what you want to achieve, you can concentrate on the important things by prioritising and focusing.

Goal setting gives you long term-vision and short-term motivation.

SMART GOALS ARE

SPECIFIC, MEASURABLE, ATTAINABLE, RELEVANT, TIMELY

You can write your goals using this approach, or just write a simple goal.

Writing Exercise #14
How are you going to do this?
Write down your goal for learning to manage your emotions.

For example: If I get annoyed with my brother, I am going to calmly walk to my room and listen to my favorite music instead of having a fight with him.

Your goal for learning to manage your emotions.

SKILL 2

FLEXIBLE THINKING

A. THE PROCESS FOR FLEXIBLE THINKING

WHAT IS FLEXIBLE THINKING?
To solve a problem, you need to have a process:

1. Figure out **what** the problem is
2. Have a think of some **options** for how to solve the problem
   this is where we come to flexible thinking.
3. Make the **best choice** from the options

Flexible thinking is remembering that there is almost always more than one way to solve a problem.

Remember the Logical Brain handles the problem solving by looking at several solutions and picking the best one.

Flexible thinking is always keeping an open mind.

The way you start out thinking may be a good solution, but another way may be better. It doesn't mean your first way is the wrong way, it means that the other way may be better suited to solve the problem—it may be quicker or easier.

Keep an open mind and be flexible.

Writing Exercise #15
What does Flexible Thinking mean to you?

Have a think about "Flexible Thinking."
We could also say that it's like "Having a choice".

What does Flexible Thinking mean to you?

B. SOLVING PROBLEMS AND FLEXIBLE THINKING

WHAT IS PROBLEM SOLVING?

It's easy to look at problems as if they are too hard to deal with, and so you just push them aside and move onto the next thing.

But there lies the problem. If you don't solve the problem, it will just come back again and again until you figure out a way to fix it or solve it.

Solving a problem is connecting back to our Logical Brain—don't become stressed, be calm and work through options to find a solution.

Writing Exercise #16
Solving a problem

Have a think about how you solve problems. Do you just wait for them to go away? Does that work? Do you use flexible thinking? Do you use the first solution without considering other options? Write down how you would usually solve problems.

Writing Exercise #17
Other people and their thinking

Sometimes people get very stuck in their way of thinking.
This is "All-or-Nothing" Thinking. If you are in a situation where someone is using "All-or-Nothing" Thinking - you will now be able to recognise it.

Think of someone in your life who often uses "All-or-Nothing" Thinking. Write an example of what he or she would say

Example: "You're always telling me what to do!"
(Hmmm Would this be using Flexible Thinking or "All-or-Nothing" Thinking?)

In the coming weeks

Notice if anyone uses "All-or-Nothing" Thinking,
but also notice if you're using "All-or-Nothing" Thinking.

C. "ALL-OR-NOTHING" THINKING OR FLEXIBLE THINKING?

Be patient and flexible instead of impatient and inflexible.

It's natural to be impatient and inflexible when you're a child. A child wants what they want and they want it now. As you grow older, you can learn to become more and more patient and flexible. This helps you accomplish more or more things, because so many things take time. But this takes practice.

In the future, instead of striving to get what you want right away, it's more appropriate to be flexible. Maybe it might take a little more time to achieve the outcome that you want. That's ok, have patience. Understanding that it might take a bit more time is thinking flexibly.

COMPARING "ALL-OR-NOTHING" PROBLEMS AND LOGICAL SOLUTIONS
Write some of your own solutions to these problems:

PROBLEM	LOGICAL SOLUTIONS
I don't know how to do my maths home-work? I just won't do it!	An example of using Flexible Thinking: Maybe I could ask someone for some help.
My parents are always asking me to clean up my room, and do chores around the house, but I don't want too.	
I have a party this weekend that I really want to go too, but my parents have said I have to go with them to a family get together. I'm just not going.	

Writing Exercise #18
Solving problems

Think about one problem you've had in the last few weeks.
Write down three possible solutions.

For example: My problem is that I want to have a gathering at my house – about 20 people. My parents have said NO.
(If you can't think of one – use the example used above and write some flexible thinking solutions below.)

PROBLEM

1

2

3

Solving problems

Think about another problem you've had in the last few weeks. Write down three possible solutions.

PROBLEM

1

2

3

Solving problems

Think about another problem you've had in the last few weeks.
Write down three possible solutions.

PROBLEM

1

2

3

D. WAYS OF USING FLEXIBLE THINKING

THERE IS ANOTHER WAY
When communicating or discussing things with your friends or family or your teacher, some people may disagree with you and you might get upset.

Don't get stuck in defensive thinking—this is your Reaction Brain reacting. Remember, by using flexible thinking it could lead to opportunities that you might not have come across unless you changed your way or view of looking at something.

Sometimes it helps to say:

> I hadn't looked at it that way before. I'll have to think about it.

BILL'S EXAMPLE
Once Bill was teaching a large group of people and one of them angrily disagreed with something he said. At first Bill started feeling angry about being attacked in front of a large group and he believed that he was right on the issue. But then he quickly said: "I hadn't looked at it that way before. I'll have to think about it." The person immediately quieted down and Bill went on with what he was saying.

After the program was over, a woman told Bill that the biggest thing she was going to remember from his talk was how he calmly responded to the person who criticized him. (She didn't know that he had been practicing for this type of situation.)

Did Bill use managed emotions or flexible thinking or both in that situation?

Writing Exercise #19
Solving a problem

In what ways can you better use flexible thinking when talking with other people? Perhaps with your teacher? Your parents? Let's look at when you're asked to do something that you don't want to do. Instead of just saying "I don't want to do that," what could you say?

Write down what a Flexible Thinking response might be below.

> **For example:** Your teacher asked you to assist her with a job at lunch time.
> You just want to chill and hang out with your friends.
> A flexible thinking response might be: "Ok sure, I can hang out with my friends tomorrow."

In what ways can you better use flexible thinking when talking with other people? Perhaps with your teacher? Your parents? Let's look at when you're asked to do something that you don't want to do. Instead of just saying "I don't want to do that," what could you say?

Write down what a Flexible Thinking response might be below.

In what ways can you better use flexible thinking when talking with other people? Perhaps with your teacher? Your parents? Let's look at when you're asked to do something that you don't want to do. Instead of just saying "I don't want to do that," what could you say?

Write down what a Flexible Thinking response might be below.

E. MAKING PROPOSALS

Another way to use your flexible thinking is to make a proposal or suggestion. When you do this, you are using your Logical Brain because you can think of several different options and then turn one into your proposal and tell others what it is.

EXAMPLE

> I propose (or suggest) that we practice football after school on Wednesday on the Lindsey Field.

Proposals usually contain at least four details:
WHO does **WHAT, WHERE** and **WHEN.**
Does this suggestion contain all four of those?

PROPOSALS ARE GOOD because they focus people's attention on the future instead of the past. You can even use proposals to get out of an argument about the past.

EXAMPLE

> You never cared about practicing, which is why we keep losing our games. It's all your fault!

Instead of arguing and saying that's not at all true you could say:

> I propose that we practice football after school on Wednesday on the Lindsey Field.

It switches the whole conversation from blaming to problem-solving.

USING PROPOSALS TO MAKE DECISIONS

We have a 3-step method for using proposals to make decisions, large and small.

1. One person makes a proposal
(Who does what, where & when)

2. Other person(s) ask questions
First person answers them

By asking questions, it keeps people from just rejecting the proposal, especially if they're upset with the proposal. Instead, it pushes everyone to use their Logical Brain by thinking of questions and answers.

One of the best questions is to ask "What would your proposal look like in action?" This way you can get clearer on the **Who, What, Where and When** of the proposal. **You might even ask:** "What's your picture of how this would work? What would you do? What would I do, if you could picture your proposal actually happening?"

3. Other person(s) say

Yes — Means you have an agreement, a plan. Work out the details and do it. Yay!

No — Simply means you need to make a new proposal or suggestion. Keep making proposals until you can both agree on something.

I'll think about it — Is a good answer because that means it is being taken seriously, but the person needs more time or needs to get more information.

In a tense situation, this often relieves the tension so that everyone can keep using their Logical Brain—which works a little slower than the Reaction Brain.

Agree on how much time the person needs to think about it.

EXAMPLE: TWO SIBILINGS ARE SHARING A BICYCLE

> I want to use the bike all day on Saturday to go on a long ride with my friend.

That's ridiculous! You know I like to go to the hobby store on Saturday afternoons.

> Please, just ask me questions first.

Oh, that's right.
Okay, when would you leave the house in the morning and when would you get back from your ride?

> I'm planning on leaving at 8am. I should be back by about 3pm.

Oh really? If you're back right at 3pm, then I can still get to the hobby store for what I want before they close at 5. But can I be sure you'll get back in time. If you're not back, what can we do?

> I'm sure I'll be back on time. But if I'm not, You can have it all day next Saturday. How's that?

Let me think about it. *makes a phone call*

5 Minutes Later

Okay, it's a deal. But you better be back on time!

> Thanks! Don't worry.

Writing Exercise #20
Proposals and questions

What do you think of how the two sibilings made their decisions?
Did they use the 3-step proposal method? How were the proposals presented?
Write down which steps you think they used.

Proposals and questions

Think of a proposal (suggestion, idea, something you want, etc.) that you would like to make to somebody. Write out how you would like the conversation to go along the lines of the conversation between the two sibilings.

Proposals and questions

Ask someone else if they can spot the 3 steps in the proposal conversation you wrote on the left. Do you think that using this approach can be helpful, especially when two people start out arguing? Write down why you think this would work or wouldn't work in your situation.

F. GOAL SETTING FOR FLEXIBLE THINKING

Hopefully you've learnt that Flexible Thinking will help you to be open minded and "All-or-Nothing" Thinking will keep you close minded. It will close the door on your ability to cope with change.

Opportunities and changes will arise in your life all the time, and if you use "All-or-Nothing" Thinking you may miss these opportunities.

Having a goal for flexible thinking will assist you to be open-minded.

Sometimes other people's ideas or thoughts might just be a better way than my idea or what I was thinking.

Writing Exercise #21
What is your Flexible Thinking goal?
What is a goal that will help you to become more flexible in your thinking?

For example: I want to use more flexible thinking in making plans with my friends.

Sometimes other people's ideas or thoughts might just be a better way than my idea or what I was thinking.

What is your Flexible Thinking goal?

SKILL 3

MODERATE BEHAVIOR

A. AVOID OVERREACTING

WHAT IS OVERREACTING?
It's acting in an unacceptable way that doesn't fit the situation. It's behavior like yelling, throwing things, hitting things, hitting someone, hiding, running away, and so on. It's having unmanaged emotions and not being in control of your emotions, so that they drive you to act in ways that are extreme and don't fit. It's acting before stopping and thinking. It's not calming your upset emotions before you go too far.

In many ways, overreacting is taking actions that would fit if it really was a crisis (like running, yelling, hitting to protect yourself), when it's not really a crisis. It's acting in a way that is exaggerated for the problem situation.

It helps to look at the connection between our thinking, feeling and acting. Often our thinking influences our feelings, which influence how we act, like this:

$$\text{Thoughts} \\ \downarrow \\ \text{Feelings} \\ \downarrow \\ \text{Actions}$$

It's almost like dominoes, **one triggers the next**—of course, we usually aren't even aware that this is what's happening —it can be so fast and not even conscious.

EXAMPLES

You were just told that you couldn't spend the night with a friend because you were behind on your homework.

Suppose you were so angry that you threw a cell phone across the room and cracked the screen. Here's what this looks like:

OVERREACTING
"It's not fair!
I really want this person to like me!
This is a crisis!"

↓

"Now I'm really angry"

↓

Throws cell phone across room.

Now, suppose you told yourself: "This isn't a crisis. We'll get together another day. If they're really my friend, we'll get another chance."

NOT OVERREACTING
"This isn't a crisis!"

↓

"I'm upset,
but now I'm calming down."

↓

"I feel like throwing
my phone across room,
but I won't do it."

SOMETIMES JUST ASKING YOURSELF:

> # Is this really a crisis?

will help you avoid overreacting.

ANOTHER EXAMPLE

OVERREACTION SITUATION

I yelled at my mom because she wouldn't take me to the shops to buy some new shoes

FEELINGS YOU WERE EXPERIENCING

Jealous. Angry. Hurt. Frustrated. Resentful.

THOUGHTS YOU WERE HAVING

I had free dress day the next day and I wanted new shoes because Sarah had new shoes.

NEW WAYS FOR LIFE → YOUTH JOURNAL

Writing Exercise #22
Did I overreact?
Think of two extreme behaviors that you used and regretted afterwards, once you eventually calmed down your upset emotions.

1

2

Writing Exercise #23
How did I overreact?

In the two situations you listed in the previous question, have a think about what extreme thoughts you were thinking and feelings you were acting on?

Maybe your behavior was driven by anger, sadness or frustration? Or maybe you were having a real mixture of emotions – sad, frustrated and overwhelmed.

Some feelings you might have been feeling at the time: Overwhelmed, sad, frustrated, angry, disgusted, fear, shame, jealous, suspicious, envious or anxious

Take a moment to think about these thoughts you were having and feelings you were experiencing and write them below.

FEELINGS YOU WERE EXPERIENCING	THOUGHTS YOU WERE HAVING

B. MODERATE BEHAVIORS

WHAT IS MODERATE BEHAVIOR?
It's acting in a way that fits the situation; that's socially acceptable. It's about keeping your thinking flexible and managing your emotions. Being calm and rational in your reactions in most situations. It's how most people act when it isn't a crisis.

WHAT IS EXTREME BEHAVIOR?
This is behavior that doesn't fit the situation; that's not socially acceptable. Examples would be stealing someone's property, yelling at a friend in public, running out of a room because you didn't like what you heard, or spreading rumours about someone that you know aren't true.

What are five examples of Extreme Behavior that you can think of?

1

2

3

4

5

Writing Exercise #24
Moderate and Extreme Behaviors.

For some EXTREME behaviors		think of better MODERATE behaviors
EXAMPLE: Punching	$\longrightarrow$	Going for a walk if I'm upset

Writing Exercise #25
What did you learn about Moderate and Extreme Behaviors

Writing Exercise #26
My Moderate and Extreme Behaviors
Think of two future situations where you may feel like acting or reacting with extreme behavior.

Write the behavior you might feel like doing, and then write what an alternative might be if you were to use moderate behavior or moderate response instead.

C. SENDING TEXT MESSAGES AND WRITING EMAILS

SENDING TEXTS
Let's face it, we all send text messages.
According to statistics in the USA: females 13 to 17 year olds send a whopping 4,050 texts per month while males aged 13 to 17 years send a tad lower at 2,539. How do you think the USA stacks up against Australian 13 -17 year olds? We would think not far behind!

Writing Exercise #27
Responding to nasty or hurtful texts!
Have you ever received nasty or hurtful text messages on messenger, Whatsapp, Instagram or Facebook? If so, how do you usually respond to the other person's personal attacks and potentially inaccurate message? What are some of the things you have said?

WRITING EMAILS

Emails are great for sending information or updates, but they are not so great when you open an email and find that someone is being nasty, perhaps for no reason at all or they have inaccurate information.

(Emails are probably not something you do that often, but you will in the future.)

Writing Exercise #28
Responding to nasty emails

Have you ever received nasty emails? If so, how do you usually respond to the other person's personal attacks and inaccurate information? What are some of the words you have used?

THE BIFF METHOD®

The BIFF Communication Method was developed to give a Moderate response to hostile or misinformed emails and other writings. This is one of the biggest areas these days where Extreme behavior comes out a lot.

THE BIFF METHOD HAS FOUR CHARACTERISTICS

B

BRIEF. By only writing 2-4 sentences, you don't give the other person much to react to or criticize.

A BIFF response can fit with any writing you receive of any length. Four pages of hate mail? Just respond with 2-4 sentences. Two sentences of accusations? Just 2-4 sentences for the response.

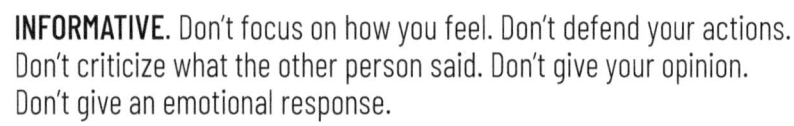

I

INFORMATIVE. Don't focus on how you feel. Don't defend your actions. Don't criticize what the other person said. Don't give your opinion. Don't give an emotional response.

Just provide some factual, objective information on whatever the topic is. This puts your response into their Logical Brain, rather than triggering their Reactive Brain unnecessarily.

F

FRIENDLY. A friendly greeting or brief cheerful comment or closing in your BIFF can help the other person calm down.

You don't have to be super friendly, but it helps to keep the tone somewhat friendly so you don't trigger their Reactive Brain unnecessarily.

F

FIRM. This doesn't mean harsh. It just means that you try to end the conversation rather than keeping it going back and forth with nasty comments.

Sometimes you might need some information or a decision from the other person. In that case, try to put it into a question that they can answer with a Yes or No response.

Also, ask for a response by a certain day and time, otherwise they may never respond.

LET'S SUPPOSE YOU GOT A TEXT LIKE THIS

> I can't believe you "used" me to help you with your math homework and didn't help me with anything at all. It was all one-way your way!
> I don't want to study together anymore!

WOULD THE FOLLOWING BE A BIFF RESPONSE?

> Thanks for letting me know.
> I appreciated your help. I thought I helped you with your little brother at your house last week.
> Let's stop studying together but still be friends.

IS THIS RESPONSE...

BRIEF?
Yes
It was just four sentences

INFORMATIVE?
Yes.
Apreciation is shown
Reciprocation (help with brother) is mentioned
None of that is defensive, emotional, or opinion focused
Just straight information
There's no reaction to the anger at all

FRIENDLY?
Yes
Best intentions and friendship wishes are expressed

FIRM?
Yes
The conversation was ended with hope
instead of arguing.

AS AN ALTERNATIVE YOU CAN ASK

> If you want to get together to talk about this, let me know.

D. PRACTICE SENDING TEXT MESSAGES WITH BIFF

Sometimes we get a text (or any social media) that is hurtful and all we want to do is send back an equally hurtful text. It might make you feel good for a moment, however, it will generally make things worse.

THINK FOR A MOMENT
If you receive a nasty or hurtful text, you could respond with a nasty or hurtful one back. What do you think will happen? The messages will get nastier and more hurtful each time you go back and forth. (This is Extreme behavior.)

However, if you didn't respond at all—you would instantly stop the back and forth. (This would be considered as Moderate behavior.)

OR GIVE A BIFF RESPONSE.
It's the same for responding to emails.
Keep it Brief, Informative, Friendly and Firm.

Writing Exercise #26
Practice responding with BIFF texts
You received this text:

> You're so weird. Get a life.

Which of these is using a BIFF response?
- ○ If you don't have anything nice to say, please stop texting me.
- ○ F off
- ○ You're the one that's weird. You need a life!
- ○ Please stop texting me. Thank you.

Write below your preferred BIFF response:

Writing Exercise #26
Your BIFF response text
Look at your response above. Do you think you should make any changes? If so, write your new response below or think of another way to respond and write it below. Talk it over with someone else.

E. 10 BIFF RESPONSE QUESTIONS TO ASK YOURSELF

What to ask yourself when writing a BIFF response:

1. Is it BRIEF?
2. Is it INFORMATIVE?
3. Is it FRIENDLY?
4. Is it FIRM?
5. Does it contain advice?
6. Are you being nasty?
7. How do you think the other person will respond?
8. If you received this message, how would you feel?
9. Is there anything you would take out, add or change?
10. Should I get a friend to read it first?

Writing Exercise #31
Review your recent texts
Think about some of your recent texts and review them with the 10 BIFF Questions. Check your phone and see what you can find.

How can you make your own texts or email responses mirror that of a BIFF Response?
Maybe you could make them a little firmer. Maybe a bit more friendly. You may want to remove anything nasty or hurtful. It may not be brief. Write down a few changes you think you can make in the future, so that your texts look like a BIFF response.

Writing Exercise #32
Using BIFF responses
In the next week, remind yourself to use a BIFF response when you send a text or respond to one that might be not very nice. **How will you remind yourself to do this?**

Writing Exercise #33

What was the most helpful part of this section on Moderate Behaviors?

How can you avoid overreacting?

What was the most helpful part of learning these skills to avoid overreacting?

Writing Exercise #34
How can you use what you've learned about Moderate Behavior in your life?

Maybe it's behaving moderately when you feel angry, maybe it's responding moderately to an email or text or maybe it's responding moderately to your parents decision when you can't go to the party that you would like to go to.
Write down a few ideas below

F. GOAL SETTING FOR MODERATE BEHAVIOR

Having a goal will help you get to an end result.

Think about a moderate behavior goal for the coming week, or for the next few weeks, that you want to work on, so your behavior can be managed. It may be a face to face situation that you will be dealing with or it could be with family members.

The goal is to think flexibly, manage your emotions, and use moderate behavior.

Writing Exercise #34
What is your Moderate Behavior goal?
Write down a difficult situation and how you will use moderate behavior.

What is your Moderate Behavior goal?

SKILL 4

CHECKING YOURSELF

It's easy to revert into old ways, but now you have some pretty amazing life skills to use each and every day.

"Checking Yourself" is all about pulling these skills together. It also helps you to avoid being preoccupied with blaming others.

Check-in with yourself. It doesn't take long to realise that you aren't managing your emotions or that you are perhaps over-reacting and you're not compromising on your one eyed view of the situation.

Writing Exercise #36
How do I check myself?

Have a think about the phrase you wrote down about calming yourself with encouraging statements.
This is the time to check yourself.
You'll need to manage your emotions, think flexibly and use moderate behavior!
Can you think of a time that you might need to check yourself in the coming weeks?
Write down when you think you might need to Check yourself.

In the next week, you may be put in a situation that requires checking yourself. What are some ways you can remember to use this skill?

Writing Exercise #37
Checking your behavior using these skills
By now we really hope that you would be able to demonstrate the 4 Big Skills: **Managed Emotions, Moderate Behavior, Flexible Thinking** and **Checking Yourself.** You can start to use these skills at home, at school, when playing sport, with your family. Have a think of other places you could use them.
Write down how knowing these skills will impact your future?

Share your statement with someone else.

Writing Exercise #38
Checking Yourself for not blaming others

Suppose you had an argument with a friend at their house and then you suddenly said the following:

> You're no good! You're a terrible friend.
> I'm never going to talk to you again.

And then you stormed out of their house. After you got away, you calmed down and realized you should check yourself.

How did this statement fit with The 4 Big Skills we have been talking about in this journal?

Managed Emotions

Flexible Thinking

Moderate Behavior

Checking Yourself

Suppose you decided to call your friend and
Say something that demonstrated Flexible Thinking, Managed Emotions and Moderate Behavior

What would you say:

CONGRATULATIONS!

You have finished your journal.

Now you can practice using these skills every day.

Remember to Check Yourself, because nobody is perfect.

We all can learn to do better and better, based on our life experience.

Now you have 4 Big Skills for Life!
BEST WISHES FROM BOTH OF US!

Notes

Notes

Notes

FEELINGS WORD GUIDE

At any time, you can check yourself for how you are feeling. You can use the list below. When you have an upset feeling, sometimes it helps to just be able to say the word that goes with the feeling. Then it's not as powerful over your life.

You can use positive words to help give yourself an encouraging statement.

CALM	HAPPY	HURT	CHERISHED
LONELY	HOPEFUL	IGNORED	APPRECIATED
OVERJOYED	DESPAIR	JUDGED	UNDERSTOOD
DISAPPOINFED	SAD	REJECTED	EMPOWERED
BITTER	OPTIMISTIC	OFFENDED	ACCEPTED
SORROWFUL	ENTHUSIASTIC	DESTROYED	HEALED
UPSET	THRILLED	HATED	LOVED
ANGRY	LOVING	DESPISED	REASSURED
DISGUST	KIND	CRUSHED	SAVED
HATEFUL	AMUSED	MISTREATED	COMMENDED
DEPRESSED	SUPPORTED	FORGOTTEN	ESTEEMED
WEAK	STRONG	BORED	DETERMINED
HOPELESS	COMFORTED	DRAINED	REFRESHED
SCARED	RELAXED	FATIGUED	ALERT
ANXIOUS	ENCOURAGED	POWERLESS	INVIGORATED
PRESSURED	ASSURED	EXHAUSTED	CREATIVE
NERVOUS	PREPARED	SICK	HEALTHY
WORRIED	FORGIVEN	PARALYSED	INSPIRED
EMBARRASSED	BEAUTIFUL	INDIFFERENT	MOTIVAFED
STRESSED	CENTAINTY	WEARY	REJUVENATED
WORTHLESS	BRAVE	STALE	FOCUSED
GUILTY	VALUED	DEJECTED	RENEWED

CPSIA information can be obtained
at www.ICGtesting.com
Printed in the USA
JSHW020418310720
6941JS00001B/2